KOREAN WAR MEMORIAL

HISTORIC LANDMARKS

Jason Cooper

The Rourke Book Company, Inc.
Vero Beach, Florida 32964

© 2001 The Rourke Book Company, Inc.

PHOTO CREDITS:
All photos © Mae Scanlan

PRODUCED & DESIGNED by East Coast Studios
eastcoaststudios.com

EDITORIAL SERVICES:
Janice L. Smith for Penworthy Learning Systems

Library of Congress Cataloging-in-Publication Data

Cooper, Jason, 1942-
    The Korean War Memorial / Jason Cooper.
        p. cm. — (Historic Landmarks)
    Includes index.
    ISBN 1-55916-327-5
    1. Korean War Veterans Memorial (Washington, D.C.)—Juvenile literature.
2. Korean War, 1950-1953—Juvenile literature. [1. Korean War Veterans Memorial
(Washington, D.C.) 2. Korean War, 1950-1953. 3. National monuments.] I. Title.

DS921.92.U6 C66 2000
951.904'26—dc21

                                              00–039004

Printed in the USA

TABLE OF CONTENTS

THE KOREAN WAR MEMORIAL

The Korean War Memorial in Washington, D.C., remembers a sometimes forgotten war.

The memorial was officially opened in 1995. It honors the 1.5 million Americans who served in Korea during the war.

The Korean War began in 1950 and ended in 1953. It was a costly and bloody war in a distant Asian country.

The Korean War Veterans Memorial honors Americans who defended "a country they never knew and a people they never met".

The Korean War started just 5 years after a much bigger conflict, World War II (1939-1945). And soon after the war in Korea ended, America's 10-year war in Vietnam began. Sandwiched between a larger war and a longer war, the Korean war was often overlooked.

But in 1986 the United States Congress agreed to build a memorial to **veterans** (VET uh runz) of the Korean War. The project finally began in 1993.

The Pool of Remembrance stands in a grove of trees at the Memorial.

THE KOREAN WAR

After World War II ended, Korea was divided. North Korea formed a **communist** (KAHM yuh nist) government, like that of nearby Russia and China. South Korea had a more **democratic** (deh muh KRAH tik) government, like that of the United States.

On June 25, 1950, North Korean soldiers poured into South Korea. The organization of countries called the United Nations was shocked at North Korea's attack. Led by the United States, the U.N. immediately sent thousands of soldiers to South Korea's defense.

Stainless steel figures by World War II veteran Frank Gaylord help show the Korean War experience of American soldiers.

9

By the end of June, the North Koreans had captured South Korea's capital city, Seoul. But U.S. and U.N. forces soon turned the flow of battle. One U.N. army fought in southern South Korea. Meanwhile, American General Douglas MacArthur landed a second U.N. force north of Seoul, at Inchon. By September 26, the Allies—U.N. and South Korean forces—had retaken Seoul. Now the Allies moved northward and captured Pyongyang, North Korea's capital. Then they moved deeper into North Korea. They marched toward the Yalu River, the border between China and North Korea.

The Korean War Veterans Memorial shows foot soldiers on patrol. A fiery air war took place in Korea, too, as both sides sent jets into the skies.

When the fighting ended in 1953, General MacArthur was out of uniform. He had been fired early in the war by President Harry Truman because MacArthur had wanted to attack China.

MacArthur's actions, the President thought, risked a larger war which might involve both China and Russia as allies of North Korea.

China was not pleased. It sent thousands of its soldiers into the fighting in October and November. The Chinese pushed the Allies south. The Chinese retook Pyongyang and marched back into South Korea. By January, the communist forces of China and North Korea had retaken Seoul.

Then, once again, the war's direction changed. The Allies built up their armed forces. They retook Seoul without a fight in March 1951. Soon both sides had dug into the hills near the 38th Parallel. That was the imaginary line that divided North and South Korea.

One of the steel patrol soldiers holds a two-way radio. Such radios allowed field patrols to keep in contact with their support commands.

The war continued in the hills for 2 more years. Peace talks began in July 1951, but the sides couldn't agree on prisoner exchanges. Finally, in July 1953, they stopped fighting and agreed on prisoner exchanges.

The war had killed about 1 million South Korean **civilians** (suh VIL yunz) and 580,000 Allied soldiers. Another 1.6 million North Koreans and Chinese had been killed or wounded.

The soldiers' heavy ponchos offered some protection from the bitter Korean winters.

The peace settlement left the line between the 2 Koreas near the 38th Parallel. It was very close to where it had been when the war began! There were still 2 Koreas.

The peace talks ended the fighting, but they didn't settle the differences between the Koreas. American soldiers are still in South Korea. A real agreement for lasting peace has never been signed between North and South Korea.

*The juniper plants at the statues'
feet recall the low, coarse plants of
Korean battlefields.*

VISITING THE MEMORIAL

The Korean War Memorial has several parts. A Triangular Field of Service has 19 steel statues created by Frank Gaylord. The statues represent a squad of American soldiers in wartime Korea. The steel soldiers are from the U.S. Air Force, Army, Marines, and Navy.

A granite curb north of the steel soldiers lists 22 countries. These countries sent soldiers or medical help to South Korea.

Nearly as many U.S. servicemen died in Korea as in the much longer Vietnam conflict. The popular TV show M.A.S.H. was set in Korea during the war.

DEAD
U.S.A. 54,246   U.N. 628,833

A black granite wall east of the soldiers has been carved with soldiers' faces. The nearby Pool of Remembrance is circled with trees. The number of those killed, wounded, missing and once held as prisoners of war is marked in stone. Opposite the numbers is a granite wall with this message: "Freedom is Not Free."

GLOSSARY

civilian (suh VIL yun) — one who is not part of a nation's military forces

communist (KAHM yuh nist) — one who belongs to the Communist part, known for its strong central government and control over individual freedoms

democratic (deh muh KRAH tik) — referring to those things that are decided by the will of the majority of people; open and free

veterans (VET uh runz) — those who have been members of the armed forces, such as a U.S. Navy veteran

INDEX

FURTHER READING

Find out more about the Korean War Memorial and the Korean War with these helpful books and information sites:

McGowen, Tom. *The Korean War.* Franklin Watts, 1993.

Korean War Memorial
   www.nps.gov/kwvm